D0753546

The
RALPH
NADER
and Family
COOKBOOK

The
RALPH
NADER
and Family
COOKBOOK

Classic Recipes from Lebanon and Beyond

BROOKLYN, NEW YORK, USA
BALLYDEHOB, CO. CORK, IRELAND

All rights reserved. No part of this book may be reproduced, stored in a retrieval system, or transmitted in any form, by any means, including mechanical, electronic, photocopying, recording, or otherwise, without the prior written consent of the publisher.

All food photography by Wendy Pernerewski
Design and layout by Sohrab Habibion

Published by Akashic Books
©2020 Ralph Nader

ISBN: 978-1-61775-794-5
Library of Congress Control Number: 2019949595

All rights reserved
First printing

Printed in Malaysia

Akashic Books
Brooklyn, New York, USA
Ballydehob, Co. Cork, Ireland
Twitter: @AkashicBooks
Facebook: AkashicBooks
E-mail: info@akashicbooks.com
Website: www.akashicbooks.com

YOU ARE URGED TO PURCHASE ORGANICALLY CERTIFIED FOOD WHENEVER POSSIBLE

INTRODUCTION

I grew up in Winsted, Connecticut, a small factory town nestled in the Litchfield Hills and lake country, surrounded by farms. It was an accepted practice that the fresh foods prepared for our meals were to be consumed without any whining or puckered facial expressions. My mother and father and their four children—two girls and two boys—all ate the same food. There were no food clashes; there was peace and time for what our parents wanted us to discuss, inform, and question regarding our schooling and readings.

However, one day my eight-year-old self rebelled. My mother Rose gave me a plate of fresh radishes, celery, and carrots.

"I don't want that," I said.

"Now, eat your food, it's very good for you," she replied.

"I don't like it."

"Ralph," she urged, "these vegetables will make you stronger and a faster runner." She nudged the dish closer to me.

"No, no, Mother, I don't want to eat it."

A triple rejection was very, very rare in our household. Mother did not believe in coerced or incentive-driven food consumption. She leaned over with her warm smile and asked: "Ralph, when you say *I don't like* or *I don't want to eat*, who is *I?*"

A little flustered, I blurted out, "*I?* It's me, Ralph."

"I'm not sure, son. Could it be your heart, your lungs, your liver, your kidneys that are saying no?"

By this time, I was reduced to sputtering noises.

She continued: "Ralph, I think I know who *I* might be."

"Who?"

She smiled again and said, "*I* is your tongue, which you have turned against your brain. Now, eat so you grow up healthy." Which, grudgingly, I began to do, looking forward to the tasty meal coming right after these "appetizers."

That's a glimpse of my mother's way with food. To her, food—whether at breakfast, lunch, or supper—was a daily occasion for education, for finding out what was on our minds, for recounting traditions of food, culture, and kinship in Lebanon, where she and my father were born. Nutritious food was essential, we were told, to a healthy body and mind. Our mother cooked her delicious recipes from scratch. There were no processed foods on our table. Since the family owned an eatery, bakery, and delicatessen in the middle of town, called the Highland Arms Restaurant, my father would bring home whole grains, fresh fruits, and vegetables by the bushel.

Mother's homemade bread contrasted favorably in every way with what she called "the gummy, bleached white bread" sold in the stores. Never did hot dogs cross our plates, much less bologna or Spam. She would explain, "I don't know what is in those hot dogs, and I don't trust something I don't know about."

As much as she loved us and raised us to savor self-reliance, Mother never asked her young children—Shaf, Claire, Laura, and me—what we wanted to eat, because "young children don't know what is good for them," she told us later. "They don't have to like what they eat; they just have to eat it." We were expected to eat everything on our plates. "If children find out that not eating will bring them lots of attention, then they will frustrate their parents by making a scene again and again at the dinner table," she said. But she knew that children also have an acute sense of fair play. "Parents should eat the same food as their children, no double standard."

I do not recall my father ever complaining about the food she served, other than occasionally asking that it be heated up more.

She believed "keeping it simple" and "everything in moderation" were two good guiding principles for our dinner table. It allowed her to prepare food more quickly. We were all expected to clean up afterward (though she washed the pots to her more rigorous standards).

Mother put all four children to work in our household. In the aromatic kitchen, that meant helping her with meal preparation and baking. I recall us kneading her bread dough, decorating her many ma'mools and ka'aks, while trying to keep up with her production. She would ask for help using a hand grinder to prepare the raw kibbe for baking and cooking. My sister Claire says that regularly assisting our mother taught her how to cook her recipes by osmosis. When Mother was away, I often made burghul, lentils, and other simple, delicious

dishes during my high school years. I also liked making bran muffins. As a high school junior, I baked twenty-one muffins for Claire's twenty-first birthday. She was a student at nearby Smith College at the time. My parents visited her that day and hand-delivered them to her.

Growing up in the 1930s and '40s, our visiting friends would grimace as they watched us eat laban (now simply called yogurt), hummus, or baba ghanoush. Today, these delicacies have achieved widespread recognition among many Americans (although commercial yogurt has been made too sweet for my taste). Soups, stews, and salads, and a simple dessert such as rice pudding, a fruit dish, nuts, dates, or figs—these were common table items.

During holidays or birthdays, more elaborate entrées came from Mother's busy kitchen. One of them was called sheikh al-mahshi ("the 'king' of stuffed food"), a baked eggplant stuffed with minced lamb, pine nuts, and onions, garnished with tomatoes and served on long-grain rice with a tossed salad. Every Friday we had baked fish with tarator sauce, reflective of a Christian tradition in Lebanon.

Given that our family restaurant served ice cream, we could have had it every day, but we did not. Mother believed that abundance could create problems, and that what is taken for granted becomes less appreciated. So maybe a dozen times a year we would go down to the restaurant and watch Father make ice cream. Father bought his milk for the ice cream from local dairies on hilltops so close by that we could hear the cows mooing through our windows. When the ice cream was ready, we would fill our bowls and lap it up happily. We appreciated it that much more since it wasn't an everyday occurrence.

Father also played an important role in our food life. He specialized in bringing us bushels of fresh apples, oranges, peaches, and plums. Pears we harvested from the faithful old tree in our backyard, twenty feet from our kitchen. And his favorite fruit—grapes of all kinds. My father liked to stew Granny Smith apples, cutting them into bite-size chunks. He wasn't looking to make applesauce, and he succeeded admirably with close attentiveness. In a little saucepan, he cooked the morning oatmeal with the same practice, getting it to a creamy consistency.

Seven days a week, the Highland Arms served American food. In those days, there were few ethnic restaurants aside from Italian or Chinese. Pizza hadn't even made it big yet. Patrons just had little taste or patience for new kinds of food. They stayed in a menu routine so predictable that, as a young man working in our restaurant, I could give the cook the order as soon as a regular customer sat down. Now there are far more food choices in restaurants of all ethnic backgrounds (including twenty-five Ethiopian restaurants in the Washington, DC, area alone).

The menus at the restaurant affected our eating at home mostly at breakfast—oatmeal, pastries, poached eggs, and jam. But by and large, the cuisines of America and Lebanon were worlds apart and my sisters, brother, and I greatly preferred the home-cooked meals full of garlic, mint, and the spices of our ancestors.

Of course, there were collateral benefits. Mother knew that at the kitchen table she had our undivided attention. When we came home from our nearby schools for lunch, she would relate historic sagas, like the tales of Joan of Arc. She never read to us, preferring to rely on her memory to tell stories and recite

Arabic poetry, watching the expressions on our faces closely. Coming from a vibrant oral tradition in Lebanon, she had an endless treasure trove of recollections. So much so that when we were restless or mischievous, she, along with Dad, would reprimand or chide us with proverbs. No "shut up or you'll be sorry"; instead, the wisdom of the ages wrapped up in a concise Arabic proverb disciplined and impressed us far more. As with "jokes are to words as salt is to taste," meaning: don't overdo the silliness.

At the dinner table, my mother would gently ask us what we had learned from our teachers that day at school. Clearly, small talk and gossip were not high on her agenda, though she knew those had their place.

Mother did not believe in regular snacks between meals. Occasionally, she liked to surprise us and would give us some labneh with olive oil, tucked inside whole wheat pita bread, to take to school.

Sometime in the 1970s, having seemingly run out of criticism of my consumer protection work, the *Wall Street Journal* devoted an entire editorial to how puritanical my mother was, forcing chickpea snacks on us instead of, presumably, candy. The *Journal* was particularly incensed at my mother quietly scraping the sugary frosting off birthday cakes once we had blown out the candles—a practice that had become a family joke.

Mother reacted with amusement. Cakes had plenty of sweetness, she would say, without loading up on frosting that was pure sugar. She knew that meals were about much more than food. For Mother, the family table was a mosaic of sights, scents, and tastes, of talking, teaching, and teasing, of health, culture, stimulation, and delight. For Dad, it was a time to ask us challenging questions to sharpen our minds and our independent thinking. Such as: Do the great leaders make the changes in history or do they reflect the rising pressures from people at any given time? Is it better

to buy from a local family-owned business than a large chain store? When can a revolution be called a success? What were you taught in school that you found out not to be true?

I had several inspirations for making this cookbook. One goes back many years—people always asking me what I eat, prompted in part by my work on food safety laws. Another was the remarkable response to the 1991 collection of recipes and wisdom—"food for thought"—that my parents compiled in the volume *It Happened in the Kitchen*, which was featured twice on Phil Donahue's popular TV program. Their book was a major source for this one. Finally, the growing popularity of Arab cuisine, backed by the growing scientific research into nutrition, has broadened the audience and market for what was once seen as an "exotic" menu. Diet is viewed by both consumers and physicians as more and more significant in an individual's weight, energy level, and overall health. Medical schools, which traditionally haven't featured nutrition very prominently in their curricula, are coming around to this realization.

As is reflected in the recipes chosen for this book, we were mostly raised with Arab cuisine—more specifically the food of the people who lived in the mountains of Lebanon. Today's nutritionists have pronounced this Mediterranean diet to be just about the healthiest diet in the world. It is heavy with varieties of vegetables, fruits, grains, nuts, spices, lean but not too much red meat, mostly lamb. The noted national dish of Lebanon—kibbe—often takes center stage on the table.

Two of the recipes in this book were contributed by Chef George Noujaim, a Lebanese immigrant who runs Noujaim's Bistro and a catering service in my family's hometown of Winsted. *Connecticut Magazine* named Noujaim's the best Mediterranean restaurant in the state.

Many of the ingredients for these recipes can be found these days in general supermarkets, as well as in health food stores and specialty Mediterranean grocery stores. The recipes are healthy and are reasonably low in fat, salt, and sugar (the latter given leeway in the desserts). The dishes are easy to prepare, with only a few exceptions.

For sure, much of our upbringing happened in our comfortable kitchen—tucked between two pantries at our family table. That is why the recipes in this book evoke memories of their broader contexts and celebrate the fortune my siblings and I had of being born to such wonderful parents.

Chef George Noujaim

APPETIZERS & DIPS

"These recipes invite you to "use your own judgment,"
as my mother, Rose, would suggest. Arab food is especially suited for experimentation. Not having to follow
rigid proportions and ingredients allows you to stimulate
your own sense of ingenuity and can lead to rave
reviews from your family and guests."

HUMMUS BI TAHINI

TIME: 1 1/2 HOURS / SERVES: 6

An appetizer which can serve as a light lunch or supper. It attracts the pallet and the eye and teases the taste buds. To enhance its subtle flavor, serve at room temperature or slightly chilled. The hummus, cooked and blended smoothly, can be frozen and kept for future use. As with baba ghanoush (see page 21), hummus bi tahini works well with warmed pita bread.

ingredients

*1/2 pound dried, uncooked chickpeas
   or 3 cups of cooked chickpeas
6 cups cold water
4 garlic cloves
1 teaspoon salt
1 teaspoon cumin to taste (optional)
juice of 2–3 lemons
5 generous tablespoons tahini
2 tablespoons olive oil
1 teaspoon paprika (optional)
4–5 sprigs parsley*

DIRECTIONS

For dried chickpeas: Soak the chickpeas overnight in cold water after removing any small stones or blemished chickpeas. The next day, wash the chickpeas well, rinsing them several times.

For canned chickpeas: drain and rinse.

Put chickpeas in a pot with 6 cups of cold water and bring to a boil. Lower heat and simmer for roughly 1 hour. Tilt the cover of the pot so there is a way for the steam to escape, keeping the foam under control. The chickpeas are done when a pea can be mashed easily between two fingers.

Put garlic, salt, cumin, lemon juice, chickpeas, and tahini in a blender or food processor and blend until smooth. Follow this procedure three or four times until all the ingredients have been finely blended. If more liquid is needed, add 2 tablespoons of cold water or more lemon juice, which will give the hummus a tangy taste.

Serve on a platter chilled or at room temperature. Drizzle olive oil over the top. If you wish, you can sprinkle paprika over the hummus for color. Garnish with sprigs of parsley.

BABA GHANOUSH

TIME: 1 HOUR / SERVES: 6

Like hummus bi tahini, this appetizer can be a light meal in itself. To keep the subtle flavor of baba ghanoush, serve lukewarm or slightly chilled. After the eggplant is cooked and taken from its skin, you can freeze it for future use—adding lemon juice keeps it from darkening. My mother preferred serving this recipe fresh.

ingredients

2 medium eggplants
3 garlic cloves, or to taste
1/2 teaspoon salt
3 tablespoons tahini
juice of 3 lemons, or to taste
6–8 radishes
3–4 sprigs parsley
dash of paprika (optional)

PREPARE THE EGGPLANT

Preheat oven to 400°F.

Wash the eggplants and score them with a knife, deep enough to allow the steam to escape when baking.

Bake the eggplants in a shallow pan at 400° until the skin can be peeled off easily, about 40 minutes. Let cool.

Remove the eggplant from its skin and mash in a bowl by hand, or in a food processor for a smoother consistency.

PREPARE THE DRESSING

Peel and pound the garlic well with salt. Add tahini and mix.

Add lemon juice and mix well. Additional lemon juice gives a tart taste to the dish. Pour dressing onto eggplant and mix well.

Serve on a platter and decorate with radishes (fashioned into florets, cut into segments, or minced) and sprigs of parsley at two ends of the platter. You can also sprinkle paprika on the top for color.

LABAN
YOGURT

TIME: 5-6 HOURS / MAKES 3-4 QUARTS

Laban was a regular part of my family's diet when I was growing up and remains so. A healthy food used in a variety of recipes, or served by itself at any time.

ingredients

1 gallon whole or skim milk
4–6 generous tablespoons laban starter* (plain yogurt)

DIRECTIONS

Scald the milk over high heat in a 4-to-5-quart pot, stirring so that it does not stick. Let it rise to the edge of the pot and then remove from the heat. Cool, testing with your finger, until lukewarm.

Mix the laban starter with 2 cups of the lukewarm milk in a separate bowl, then mix back into the pot with the rest of the milk.

Cover the pot and wrap tightly with tea towels. Let sit for at least 7 to 8 hours, or overnight, on the kitchen counter.

If the laban is not quite firm enough, cover again and leave a little longer.

Refrigerate until cold, but be sure to keep it covered. The consistency, like a heavy soup, gets smoother the more you stir.

*Before serving, take a jarful of laban for use as the starter for the next time. When making for the first time, use a store-bought local organic yogurt.

LABNEH
STRAINED YOGURT

TIME: 8-9 HOURS / MAKES 2 CUPS

Labneh is a versatile spread made from laban. It is good with toast in the morning or on sandwiches. Labneh can also be mixed with dried or fresh mint and used as an appetizing dip with olive oil.

ingredients

2 quarts laban
olive oil, to drizzle (optional)
dried or fresh mint (optional)

DIRECTIONS

Place a lightly woven, unbleached muslin cloth over a strainer and pour laban into it. Then gather the cloth to cover the laban.

Put strainer over a bowl, and when the whey or liquid is drained into the bowl (you can do this overnight), the labneh should have the consistency of a creamy spread.

Serve in a glass container and drizzle a little olive oil on top along with mint.

LABAN WITH CUCUMBERS

TIME: 10 MINUTES / SERVES: 4

This dish is wonderfully tasty as an appetizer or side dish.

ingredients

5–6 garlic cloves (if you like garlic, less otherwise)
several dashes of salt
1 tablespoon dried mint
2 cucumbers, peeled and sliced
2 1/2 cups laban (see page 22)

DIRECTIONS
Pound garlic with the salt and dried mint.

Combine laban with sliced cucumbers and the garlic/dried mint mixture.

Stir well and serve cold.

SOUPS & ONE SMOOTHIE

"These soups rose to deeper levels of satisfaction during freezing New England snowstorms. As my mother once said, "These are simple foods that will warm you from the tips of your toes to the roots of your hairs and will fill the empty places between.""

LENTIL SOYBEAN SOUP

TIME: 1 1/2 HOURS / SERVES: 6

A simple, satisfying dish.

---

ingredients

1 cup soybeans
5 cups cold water
1 cup brown lentils
3 medium yellow onions, sliced
4 garlic cloves, minced
1/2 cup olive oil
3 carrots, scrubbed and cut in small
    pieces
6 celery tops
salt, pepper, and cinnamon to taste
1/2 cup fresh parsley, chopped
juice of 1 lemon

DIRECTIONS

Soak soybeans overnight in 5 cups of cold water. Save the water for cooking.

Rinse lentils.

Sauté onions and garlic in olive oil over medium heat, until onions are soft (about 5 minutes). Add soybeans, lentils, and water; bring to boil, reduce heat, and simmer for 15 minutes.

Add the carrots and celery tops.

Season to taste and simmer until carrots and celery tops are tender.

If you need to add more water for your preferred consistency, be sure to use cold water.

Garnish with parsley and the juice of one lemon.

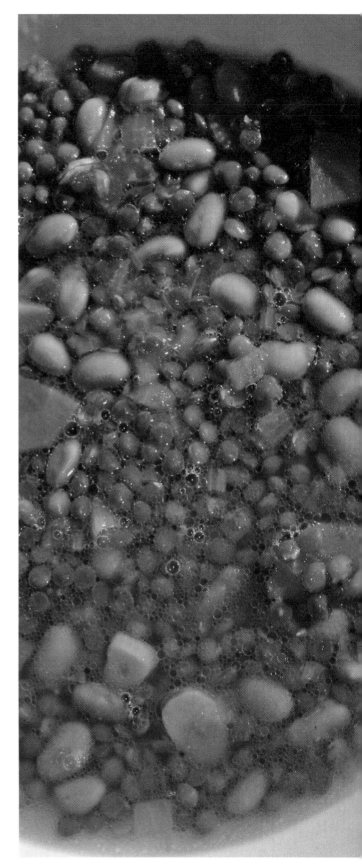

CANNELLINI BEAN SOUP WITH SWISS CHARD

TIME: 1 HOUR, 15 MINUTES / SERVES: 4-6

Cannellini beans are also known as white kidney beans.

ingredients

2 cups uncooked cannellini beans
2 large yellow onions, sliced
1/4 cup olive oil
8–10 cups water
salt and pepper to taste
5 garlic cloves, minced or whole
2 plum tomatoes, chopped into small
   pieces
1/2 teaspoon ginger powder
1/2 teaspoon turmeric powder
1/2 teaspoon curry powder
1/8 teaspoon cayenne pepper
1 bunch Swiss chard, cut into
   generous pieces

DIRECTIONS

Soak beans overnight, using enough cold water to cover them by roughly 2 inches. Rinse and set aside.

Sauté onions in olive oil in a large pot over medium heat, until soft (about 4–5 minutes).

Add beans to sautéed onions. Stir well.

Add 8 cups of water and salt and pepper to taste.

Bring to a boil. Reduce heat to medium, add garlic, and cook uncovered for about 15 minutes, until beans are half-cooked.

Add the tomatoes. Season with ginger, turmeric, curry powder, and cayenne pepper. Stir well. Reduce to simmer and cook until the beans are thoroughly done—about 30–40 minutes—and adjust spices to taste.

Add the Swiss chard, stir, remove from heat, and serve.

APPLE PARSNIP SOUP

TIME: 1 HOUR / SERVES: 4-6

---

ingredients

2 tablespoons olive oil
1 pound parsnips, peeled and diced
2 celery stalks, diced
1 medium yellow onion, diced
1/2 teaspoon cardamom
2 Granny Smith apples, peeled and diced
4 garlic cloves, sliced
4 cups chicken stock
salt and pepper to taste
1/4 cup of heavy cream
chives, chopped (to taste)

DIRECTIONS

Over medium heat, put 2 tablespoons olive oil in a large pot.

Add the diced parsnips and cook for 5 minutes until slightly softened.

Add the celery, onion, and cardamom and cook for an additional 5 minutes, stirring occasionally.

Add the apples and garlic and cook for another 5 minutes until the apples are softened.

Add the chicken stock and bring to a boil.

Reduce heat to a simmer and cook for about 20 minutes, until all the ingredients are very soft.

Remove from heat and season with salt and freshly ground pepper.

Blend until smooth.

Divide the soup into 4 to 6 bowls.

Drizzle a teaspoon of cream on top of each bowl; garnish with chopped chives.

GARLIC SOUP

RECIPE BY CHEF GEORGE NOUJAIM

TIME: 1 HOUR / SERVES: 4

---

ingredients

52 garlic cloves
1 cup olive oil
1 cup vegetable oil
1 teaspoon salt
1/2 cup dry sherry
3 cups chicken stock
2 cups heavy cream
2 scallions, chopped

DIRECTIONS

Preheat oven to 300°F.

Submerge 52 garlic cloves in a mixture of olive oil and vegetable oil. Cover and bake 30 minutes. Allow to cool. Drain the oil from the mixture.*

Put 12 garlic cloves to the side. Blend the remaining cloves until they have a paste-like consistency.

Add the garlic paste to a pot with the salt and dry sherry over low heat. Mix with a whisk until the garlic is dissolved. Add the chicken stock, bring to a boil, reduce to low, and simmer for 5 minutes.

Add the heavy cream and whisk together. Allow to simmer for another 5 minutes.

Divide the soup into 4 bowls. Add 3 of the reserved garlic cloves to each bowl. Garnish with scallions.

Tip: save flavored oil for dressings, etc.

CREAMY GINGER AND SPINACH SMOOTHIE

TIME: 5 MINUTES / YIELDS: 1 1/2 QUARTS

ingredients

2 cups spinach
1 Asian pear
1 Honeycrisp apple
1/2 avocado
1/2 cup dry sherry
1 inch fresh ginger
2 cups water

DIRECTIONS

Blend all ingredients together and serve.

SALADS

"Mother would serve us a fresh salad (salata) at dinner before the main dishes. Other parents served salads during the main meal or right afterward. It turns out that many children are more likely to eat their vegetables when served first because that's when they are most hungry. Served next to enticing chicken with fries, picky children may try to avoid vegetables."

TABOULEH

TIME: 1/2 HOUR / SERVES: 10

A refreshing, nutritious, colorful salad. Makes an elegant entrée for a summer meal. Refrigerated, tabouleh stays fresh for several days.

ingredients

3 bunches parsley
4 sprigs fresh mint
1 cup fine burghul (bulgur wheat)
2–3 bunches scallions, minced
5 tomatoes, 3 minced and 2 thinly sliced
juice of 8 lemons, or to taste
1/2 cup olive oil, or to taste
salt and pepper to taste
1 head romaine lettuce, or more if needed

DIRECTIONS

Tear parsley florets off the stems.

Pick mint leaves off the stems.

Rinse the parsley and mint.

Mince the parsley very fine and cut the mint into small pieces.

Wash burghul and soak in water for 5–7 minutes. Squeeze the water out and add to the above.

Add scallions, minced tomatoes, and lemon juice until a tart taste has been achieved. Add olive oil to taste.

Season with salt and pepper.

Wash lettuce and separate the leaves. Drain well. Place some of the lettuce leaves on a serving platter and put the tabouleh over it. Decorate the top with thin tomato slices and small pieces of lettuce all the way around the platter so that these can be included with each serving.

37

FATOOSH
TOMATOES, SCALLIONS, AND PARSLEY WITH TOASTED BREAD

TIME: 1/2 HOUR / SERVES: 6-8

A wonderful, colorful salad.

ingredients

6 slices whole wheat bread
2 tablespoons cold water
4–5 garlic cloves
2–3 cucumbers, chopped
3–4 tomatoes, the juicy variety, chopped

2–3 red and green bell peppers, chopped
1/2 head romaine lettuce, chopped or torn into small pieces
1 bunch parsley, minced, including stems
2 bunches scallions, chopped
3–4 tablespoons dried mint
juice of 3–4 lemons
1/2 cup olive oil, or to taste
salt and pepper to taste

DIRECTIONS

Toast bread and cut into small pieces.

Put toast in a bowl and sprinkle with water to moisten it somewhat; mix.

Pound garlic with 1/8 teaspoon of salt in a large bowl.

Put bread on top of the mashed garlic.

Combine chopped cucumbers, tomatoes, peppers, and lettuce with minced scallions and parsley. Put vegetables on top of the bread.

Add dried mint, lemon juice, olive oil, and salt and pepper to taste.

Toss until all the ingredients are distributed evenly.

SALATA

TOSSED SALAD

TIME: 15 MINUTES / SERVES: 4-6

This is a delicious yet simple salad; when combined with a main dish, it makes for a filling meal.

ingredients

2 garlic cloves (more if you like)
pinch of salt
1/4 cup white vinegar
  or fresh lemon juice
1/4 cup olive oil
2–3 tomatoes, chopped
1 cucumber, chopped or sliced
1 green bell pepper, chopped
1/2 bunch watercress, chopped or torn
1 1/2 heads romaine lettuce, chopped
  or torn
mint, fresh or dried

DIRECTIONS

For the dressing, pound garlic with salt and add vinegar (or fresh lemon juice) and olive oil.

Combine chopped tomatoes, cucumber, green pepper, and watercress in a bowl. (Alternatively, the cucumbers may be sliced.)

Cut or tear the lettuce into small pieces and add to the above.

About 1 hour before serving, dress the salad and add dried or fresh mint.

Cover and put in the refrigerator until time to serve. During this time the lettuce becomes even crisper and the aroma of the dressing seeps through the ingredients.

To serve, toss well so that the dressing is evenly distributed throughout the salad.

SWISS CHARD SALAD

TIME: 10 MINUTES / SERVES: 6

A refreshing, nutty, zesty salad that provides good roughage. We recommend Swiss chard that has been grown without the use of pesticides as the leaves are typically more tender.

ingredients

1 bunch Swiss chard, chopped
1/2 bunch scallions, diced
1/8 cup, or less, olive oil
1/8 cup pine nuts
salt and pepper to taste

DIRECTIONS

Wash the Swiss chard, cut into small pieces, and drain well.

Add diced scallions and pine nuts to the Swiss chard and mix well.

Dress with olive oil, and season with salt and pepper to taste.

MAIN DISHES

"Without being urged or instructed, my parents' grandchildren—Nadia, Tarek, and Rania—all taught themselves how to prepare many of the recipes in this book because they so loved the delicious flavors. Nadia's fatayer and cream cheese gelatin delight are legendary, while Tarek's tabouleh is simply unforgettable. And Rania makes the tastiest macaroon kashab; from time to time she sends packages of this delicious dessert to family members. My grandmother saw the sheikh al-mahshi dinner as a very special occasion—an "apex recipe," in today's language. The traditions continue on in our family!"

SHEIKH AL-MAHSHI
BAKED EGGPLANT STUFFED WITH LAMB AND PINE NUTS

TIME: 1 1/2 HOURS / SERVES: 6

This is the king of stuffed food and one of my favorites. Use the smallest eggplants available (very small ones are cooked whole, while medium ones, preferably on the small side, are cut in half lengthwise). Serve with long-grain brown rice.

ingredients

4 medium eggplants (or 10 small)
2 tablespoons olive oil
2 pounds ground lamb meat (boned leg of lamb, fat removed, ground at butcher or using a coarse blade on a food mill)
2 large yellow onions, diced
1/8 teaspoon cinnamon
salt and pepper to taste
2/3 cup pine nuts
4 medium tomatoes, cut in small chunks
8–10 cherry tomatoes (optional)
2 cups lamb broth
6 servings long-grain brown rice

PREPARE THE EGGPLANT
Wash and trim stems from medium eggplants. Partially peel in alternating 1-inch strips, leaving half the skin on. Cut medium eggplants in half lengthwise (leave small eggplants whole) and steam over medium heat in a covered saucepan for 15–20 minutes until the skin is soft enough that you can indent it with a poke.

Spread thin layer of olive oil onto a 9" x 13" x 2" pan. Place steamed eggplants in the pan. If using small eggplants, cut each lengthwise. Let the eggplants cool before stuffing.

PREPARE THE STUFFING
Thoroughly combine the ground lamb and onions (or grind them together in a food mill). This should make about 2 3/4 cups.

Cook the lamb and onions in a saucepan with cinnamon, salt, and pepper over low heat, stirring to avoid sticking. Add pine nuts after 5 minutes. Cook for 10–12 minutes, until the pink is gone from the lamb. Remove from heat.

PREPARE THE COMPLETED DISH
While the stuffing is cooking, gently boil the fresh tomatoes in an uncovered saucepan with 2 cups of lamb broth 10–15 minutes, until soft and juicy.

(Optional: For a decorative effect, cook the cherry tomatoes in the tomato/broth mixture to sit on top of the stuffed eggplant. Strain and set aside.)

Firmly stuff lamb filling into eggplant boats until full.

Place a generous portion of tomatoes, or cherry tomatoes, on top of each eggplant boat. Spoon tomato/broth mixture around the eggplant boats, filling pan but not overflowing eggplant. Reserve some of the liquid to add while the eggplants bake.

Bake, uncovered, at 350°F for 30–50 minutes. Add reserved broth mixture as needed.

SERVE THE EGGPLANT
Remove boat from pan and serve on a bed of long-grain rice. Top with pan drippings as desired.

SFEEHA OR FATAYER

OPEN-FACED OR STUFFED PASTRY WITH LAMB OR SPINACH FILLING

TIME: 1 HOUR PREPARATION, 20 MINUTES A TRAY TO BAKE / SERVES: 6

A most filling meal, and one of my niece Nadia's favorite dishes to bake—she baked the ones pictured here. Sfeeha is open and visibly beckons the palate. Fatayer is closed and shaped like a three-cornered hat. These are usually made with whole wheat bread dough.

ingredients for dough

1 tablespoon yeast
3/4 cup lukewarm milk (use more if
    needed to make the dough)
4 cups whole wheat flour (or 2 cups
    white and 2 cups whole wheat)

ingredients for lamb filling

2 pounds ground lamb meat (boned
    leg of lamb, fat removed, ground at
    butcher or using a coarse blade on a
    food mill)
juice of 2 lemons
2 large yellow onions, finely chopped
salt and pepper to taste
1/2 cup pine nuts (use more if
    desired)
pomegranate seeds (optional)

ingredients for spinach filling

40 ounces frozen, chopped spinach,
    thawed (or 4 lbs. fresh spinach,
    chopped)
4 tablespoons olive oil
1 yellow onion, finely chopped
salt and pepper to taste
1/2 cup pine nuts
4 tablespoons lemon juice
pomegranate seeds (optional)

PREPARE THE DOUGH

In a large bowl, dissolve yeast with 1/4 cup lukewarm milk.

Add flour; gradually add lukewarm milk and mix until a good, malleable bread dough is achieved.

Knead well by hand for about 15 minutes. Continuously dip hands in a small bowl of milk during the kneading process, wiping the side of the bowl with milk-laden hands to clean it as well. The dough should be completely mixed and glistening, and the bowl and hands clean when kneading is completed.

Cover bowl with a damp tea towel and set aside to rise. Dough should roughly double in size (45 minutes–1 hour).

Once risen, pull off small pieces of dough until you have divided it into 20 equal pieces. Roll pieces into small balls and flatten gently with your hand.

PREPARE THE LAMB FILLING AND/OR THE SPINACH FILLING

Lamb filling: thoroughly combine the ground lamb and onions (or grind them together in a food mill). Season with salt and pepper. Add lemon juice and pine nuts.

Spinach filling: Squeeze thawed spinach until you can't get much water out of it. If raw, rinse well and finely chop. Add 4 tablespoons olive oil, 4 tablespoons of lemon juice, onion, salt and pepper to taste, and pine nuts. Mix well.

PREPARE SFEEHA OR FATAYER

Preheat oven to 375°F.

To make sfeeha, flatten each ball of dough into a circle (approximately 3–4 inches wide, 1/8 inch thick) with your fingers, being careful not to flatten the edges as much as the interior. Place 3 teaspoons of uncooked filling into the center of each circle, leaving a small ring of dough around the filling. Gently press filling into dough.

To make fatayer, evenly flatten each ball of dough into a 3–4 inch circle with your fingers, and place 2 teaspoons of filling in the center. Make each into the shape of a closed three-cornered hat by pulling dough on opposite sides of the circle out and up, and pinching them together on the top and one side. Pull the remaining side of dough and pinch each edge against the rest of the circle to enclose the filling completely.

Bake for 20 minutes on a flat cookie sheet greased lightly with olive oil. Dough should be barely browned.

Sfeeha can be broiled for 1–2 minutes to make crispy.

Optional: garnish with pomegranate seeds.

BAKED KIBBE

TIME: 1 HOUR / SERVES: 8-10

Kibbe is the national dish of Lebanon—it is a favorite because of its delicate flavors and because of the variety of ways it can be prepared. It can be baked; it can be made into meat patties; it can be shaped into an egg, stuffed, and cooked in labaneeye; or it can be shaped into balls and cooked in hot broth and tomato sauce. Here we share two of our favorites.

ingredients for basic kibbe

3 pounds ground lamb meat (boned leg of lamb, fat removed, ground at butcher or using a fine blade on a food mill)
3 medium yellow onions, chopped
2 cups fine burghul (bulgur wheat)
salt and pepper to taste

PREPARE BASIC KIBBE
Thoroughly combine ground lamb and onions (or grind them together in a food mill).

Wash burghul, squeezing the water from the grain by hand.

Mix burghul with meat and onions, preferably by hand.

Season with salt and pepper.

Grind the total mixture a second time using a fine blade.

Mix with hands, using a little water to make the mixture pliable and smooth.

ingredients for kibbe filling

1/2 pound ground lamb meat (boned leg of lamb, fat removed, ground at butcher or using a fine blade on a food mill)
salt and pepper to taste
1/2 teaspoon cinnamon
1 medium yellow onion, chopped
2/3 cup pine nuts
1 teaspoon lemon juice

PREPARE FILLING
Thoroughly combine ground lamb and onions (or grind them together in a food mill).

Cook the lamb and onions in a saucepan with cinnamon, salt, and pepper over low heat, stirring to avoid sticking. Add pine nuts after 5 minutes. Cook for 10–12 minutes, until the pink is gone from the lamb. Remove from heat.

ingredients for baking

1/3 pound butter
some water for sprinkling
(continued on next page)

BAKED KIBBE

(continued from previous page)

DIRECTIONS
Preheat oven to 350°F.

Coat a 9" x 12" x 2" glass or stainless steel pan with a small amount of the butter (reserving 1/4 pound for the top of the dish).

Spread basic uncooked kibbe mixture about 1/2 inch thick, smoothing and gently pressing it down by hand; sprinkle with water. It should be very smooth.

Spread a 1/2-inch-thick layer of cooked filling over the entire pan. Pat down and gently smooth by hand.

Spread a second layer of the uncooked kibbe mixture about 1/3 inch thick. Once again, pat down and sprinkle water until very smooth.

With a wet, sharp knife, gently cut the kibbe with evenly spaced diagonal lines across the longer end of the pan and then along the shorter end, to create diamond-shaped pieces. Try to avoid disturbing the smooth surface and the filling.

With a wet knife, gently loosen the kibbe from the edges of the pan, and then score the center of each diamond-shaped piece by just inserting and removing the knife. This will allow the butter to penetrate the center of each piece.

Make a hole about the size of a nickel in the center of the dish.

Separate 1/4 pound of butter into small pieces and distribute across the top of the pan, placing some in the hole.

Bake on the bottom oven rack for 45–60 minutes, depending on the oven. The kibbe is done when you jiggle the pan and it moves.

Remove from oven, sprinkle with cold water. Cover with a tray, cookie sheet, or pan until it is served. (Kibbe can be eaten cold, but many prefer it warm right out of the oven.)

STUFFED KIBBE COOKED IN LABANEEYE

TIME: 30-45 MINUTES / SERVES 8-10

ingredients

basic kibbe mixture (see page 51)
kibbe filling (see page 51)
5–6 garlic cloves
1 teaspoon salt
mint (preferably fresh but dried is okay), use generously to taste
2 quarts laban (see page 22)
1 quart cold water
1/4 cup uncooked long-grain brown rice
1/4 teaspoon butter
1 egg
1 teaspoon salt

PREPARE STUFFED KIBBE

Place a small amount of uncooked basic kibbe mixture into the palm of your hand and shape into an oval.

While cupping and rotating the kibbe with one hand, core into the middle of the oval from the long end with the forefinger of the other hand, making a hollow space for the filling. The sides of the kibbe should be as thin as feasible. It should resemble a hollow egg.

Put about 1 teaspoon of cooked kibbe filling into the hollowed egg-shaped form. Gently close the opening or mouth, using a splash of water to smooth it closed.

DIRECTIONS FOR COOKING STUFFED KIBBE IN LABANEEYE

Pound garlic with salt and plenty of mint.

Place laban, cold water, rice, butter, salt, and egg in a large 5-quart cooking pot and cook over medium heat. (The egg is important to prevent the laban from separating when it's heated.)

With a manual egg beater (or electric one on low), beat this mixture in the pot until the labaneeye begins to boil and bubbles are evident.

When the labaneeye is boiling, add 5 or 6 stuffed kibbe (be sure they are completely closed and sealed) and cook for 2-4 minutes. The stuffed kibbe is cooked when it bounces back after being gently tapped with a spoon. It will sound hollow. Note: If the stuffed kibbe sinks when it is tapped, this means it was not completely closed and liquid has seeped inside. If this happens, simply finish cooking. It's not a disaster.

Cook the remaining stuffed kibbe, 5 or 6 at a time. Place the stuffed, cooked kibbe on a platter and cover to keep warm.

To serve, divide stuffed kibbe evenly into 8–10 soup bowls and spoon the labaneeye into each bowl.

DAJAJE MA' A' HASHWEE
CHICKEN WITH LAMB AND RICE

TIME: 1 HOUR 50 MINUTES / SERVES: 6-8

This chicken dish, dressed up with lamb, nuts, and cinnamon, has a familiar yet delightfully unique taste. It's also a low-fat, high-energy dish.

---

ingredients

1 whole chicken cut into parts (about 3 1/2 pounds)
2 teaspoons salt or more to taste
2 pounds ground lean lamb meat (boned leg of lamb, fat removed, ground at butcher or using a coarse blade on a food mill)
1/4 teaspoon cinnamon
1/4 teaspoon poultry seasoning
1/2 teaspoon cardamom
pepper to taste
1 cup long-grain rice, preferably brown
1/2 cup pine nuts
1/2 cup slivered or split blanched almonds

PREPARE THE CHICKEN
To clean chicken, cover it with cold water in a 4- or 5-quart pot with 2 teaspoons of salt and bring to a boil. After it comes to a complete boil, throw the water out, rinse the chicken, and remove its skin.

Cover chicken with cold water, about 3 inches above the chicken. Season with 1/8 teaspoon cinnamon, poultry seasoning, 1/2 teaspoon cardamom, and salt and pepper to taste. Cook uncovered and bring to boil over high heat, then reduce heat to medium low and cook for about 1 hour, until chicken pulls easily from the bone. Reserve 2–3 cups of chicken broth. Debone, keeping pieces ample, and set aside.

PREPARE THE STUFFING
Wash and drain rice. Place ground lamb, rice, pine nuts, almonds, 1/8 teaspoon cinnamon in a saucepan with reserved chicken broth, and salt and pepper to taste.

Bring to a boil, reduce heat to a simmer, cover, and cook for about 30 minutes or until rice is done and not sticking together.

TO SERVE
Mix the stuffing and the chicken pieces and serve on a large platter. Save several good-sized chicken pieces to place on top of the entire dish.

YABRAK ARISH

ROLLED STUFFED GRAPE LEAVES

TIME: 1 HOUR 35 MINUTES / SERVES: 8

Stuffed with lamb and rice, or vegetarian filling, this delicacy has become popular but it's often found in heavy olive oil. Steamed and served hot or cold, this recipe contains no added fat products. The grape leaves can be prepared ahead of time, and refrigerated or frozen uncooked, leaving out the lemon juice and water until you cook them.

---

ingredients for the main dish

1 16 oz. jar grape leaves or fresh
   grape leaves
3 large garlic cloves
3 tablespoons dried mint
salt to taste
1 cup water
juice of 2–3 lemons

---

ingredients for lamb filling

2 pounds ground lamb meat (boned
   leg of lamb, fat removed, ground at
   butcher or using a coarse blade on a
   food mill)
3/4 cup long-grain uncooked rice,
   preferably brown
salt and pepper to taste
1/8 teaspoon cinnamon

---

ingredients for vegetarian filling

1 cup long-grain uncooked rice,
   preferably brown
1 medium yellow onion, minced
1/2 cup fresh parsley, chopped
2 tablespoons fresh or dried mint
juice of 2–3 lemons

PREPARE THE LAMB AND/ OR VEGETARIAN FILLING

Lamb filling: Mix ground lamb meat with rice, season with salt, pepper, and cinnamon.

Vegetarian filling: Mix all ingredients together.

PREPARE THE STUFFED GRAPE LEAVES

Dip the grape leaves in water for about 30 seconds.

Remove stem from each grape leaf. Spread each leaf on a flat work surface. Place about 1 teaspoon of stuffing across the leaf about 1/2 inch from the stem point. Fold leaf forward toward the stuffing, then fold the right side over, then the left, and then roll the leaf forward very tightly. When fully rolled, squeeze it to secure.

Repeat this process for each leaf.

Put 4 whole grape leaves along with torn pieces of leaves on the bottom of a 5-quart pot. Neatly place each rolled stuffed grape leaf in the pot in layers.

Pound garlic with mint and salt, add 1 cup of water and lemon juice, and pour over the grape leaves in the pot. Top with several grape leaves and torn pieces. Invert a plate about the diameter of the pot on top of grape leaves to keep them firmly in place. Cover pot.

Bring to a boil, then reduce heat to a low simmer and cook for about 1 hour. Add more water if needed. Steam until grape leaves are soft and are easily pierced with a fork. Do not overcook. The leaves should not fall apart.

Cold rolled stuffed grape leaves can be reheated by steaming briefly, or eaten cold.

To serve, place on a platter in rows.

YABRAK MALFOOF

ROLLED STUFFED CABBAGE

TIME: 1 1/2 HOURS / SERVES: 6

This favorite Middle Eastern dish requires a little tender-loving effort, but the reward is in the eating.

---

ingredients

1 head green or white cabbage
2 pounds ground lamb meat (boned leg of lamb, fat removed, ground at butcher or using a coarse blade on a food mill)
3/4 cup uncooked long-grain rice, preferably brown
1 tomato chopped into small pieces
salt and pepper to taste
1/8 teaspoon cinnamon
3 large garlic cloves
3 tablespoons fresh or dried mint
juice of 3 lemons
2 cups water

DIRECTIONS

Dip cabbage in boiling water for 2 minutes, long enough to separate the leaves of the cabbage easily.

Mix ground lamb with rice and tomato; season with salt, pepper, and cinnamon.

Arrange each cabbage leaf on a worktable (cut if necessary to facilitate rolling up). Put a tablespoon of stuffing in the center of each leaf at least a half inch from the edge to permit rolling up the leaf. You may need more or less filling depending on the size of the leaf.

Start to roll, then fold right side inward and then the left side. Roll up tightly, and then squeeze in hand to seal closed. Roll up as many cabbage leaves as the filling permits.

Place about 4–6 unused cabbage leaves on the bottom of a 5-quart pot. Neatly stack rolled cabbage leaves in the pot.

Pound garlic with mint and a dash of salt, and add juice from 1 lemon. Pour over the rolled cabbage in the pot. Add 2 cups of water and top with a few unused cabbage leaves.

Invert a plate (with a diameter just smaller than the pot) over the cabbage. Cover pot.

Bring to a boil over high heat. Reduce heat to a simmer and cook slowly for about 30 minutes. Add juice from 2 lemons. Cook another 30 minutes or until the cabbage leaf is cut easily with a fork. Serve on a platter with laban.

BAKED FISH WITH SPICES AND TARATOR SAUCE

TIME: 20 MINUTES / SERVES: 4-6

Baked fish with tarator sauce is a rich and elegant way to prepare fish for a special evening.

---

ingredients for sauce

2–3 garlic cloves
1/4 teaspoon salt
1/4 cup tahini
juice of 2 lemons
2 tablespoons cold water

---

ingredients for fish

---

2 pounds of white fish fillets
   (flounder, scrod, sole, or similar)
2 lemons, sliced
salt and pepper to taste
1/8 teaspoon tarragon or curry powder
parsley to garnish

PREPARE THE SAUCE

Pound garlic with salt. Add tahini and lemon juice and mix. Add cold water as needed, mixing until smooth. Taste should be a little bit tart.

(Alternatively, use a blender to blend garlic, salt, lemon juice, and water. When mixture is smooth, blend in tahini for just a few seconds.)

PREPARE THE FISH

Preheat oven to 350°F.

Arrange slices of lemon on the bottom of a baking dish.

Place fish on top and season with salt, pepper, and either tarragon or curry powder.

Bake for 10 minutes or until fish is flaky.

Place on a platter and serve immediately with tarator sauce and parsley garnish.

BURGHUL WITH SWISS CHARD OR CHICORY

TIME: 1/2 HOUR / SERVES: 6

This recipe can be served with a tossed salad. A dollop of laban on top is also a tasty way to serve. It is a satisfying and nourishing light meal and can be prepared quickly. Cayenne pepper adds its distinctive zest.

ingredients

3 medium yellow onions, sliced
3 garlic cloves, sliced
3/4 cup olive oil
1 bunch Swiss chard or a large head of chicory
1 cup coarse burghul
1 cup water or lamb broth
1/2 teaspoon cayenne pepper
laban to taste (optional; see page 22)

DIRECTIONS

Thoroughly wash and drain the chard or chicory and chop into small pieces.

Sauté onions and garlic lightly in olive oil over low heat in a covered 3-quart pot. Lay chopped chard or chicory on top of the onions and garlic without mixing and cook covered until greens wilt.

Add the burghul and cook covered 5–6 minutes without mixing.

Mix all together and add 1 cup water or lamb broth.

Season with salt and cayenne (or black) pepper. Bring to a boil, reduce heat, and simmer, covered, until most of the liquid has been absorbed, but the dish is still moist.

Serve on a platter.

'MDARDARA

LENTILS WITH RICE AND ONION

TIME: 1 HOUR / SERVES: 8

This simple dish is rich in iron, delicious, and very filling. It makes an attractive centerpiece as a meal.

ingredients

6 medium or 3 large onions, sliced
1/2 cup olive oil
3/4 pound brown lentils
1/2 cup long-grain brown rice or
    coarse burghul
salt and pepper to taste
1/4 teaspoon cinnamon
3 cups cold water
6 large radishes, halved
1 bunch scallions, minced

DIRECTIONS

Slice and sauté onions in olive oil in a 5-quart pot until soft and slightly browned. Remove from heat and set aside half of the onions.

Wash lentils and rice (or burghul) in a bowl with cold water. Rinse several times and drain.

Add lentils, rice (or burghul), salt, pepper, cinnamon, and water to the onions in the pot. Bring to a boil, then reduce to moderate/low heat and cook until rice and lentils are dry and fluffy, but not well done, about 40 minutes.

Place 'mdardara on platter and put reserved onions on top. Sprinkle with minced scallions and evenly place radishes around the bottom edge of lentil mound for decoration.

VEGETABLES

"When I was growing up, my mother's veggie side dishes were an easy way to avoid mono-meals and stimulate a desire for a variety of nutrients and tastes. She often said that food was not simply sustenance, there was a sense of creativity in its consumption."

LOUBIEH BI ZAYT

STRING BEANS IN OLIVE OIL

TIME: 50 MINUTES / SERVES: 6 AS A
SIDE DISH, 4 AS A MAIN COURSE

*This dish goes well with fish or
served cold by itself on a hot
summer day.*

ingredients

2 pounds string beans
2 medium yellow onions, sliced
7 garlic cloves, sliced
1/4 cup olive oil
2 medium tomatoes, chopped
salt and pepper to taste

DIRECTIONS

Remove ends of beans, break in half, and
wash.

Sauté onions and garlic lightly in olive oil
and then place the string beans on top.

Place tomato pieces over the string beans.
Season with salt and pepper.

Cook on low heat for about 10 minutes,
then mix all ingredients and continue
cooking slowly until beans are tender.

BEETS WITH ONIONS IN OLIVE OIL

TIME: 45 MINUTES / SERVES: 4

This can be served warm or served cold as a refreshing summer dish. The onions provide enough seasoning, making it unnecessary to use salt.

ingredients

10 beets, skin on, scrubbed clean
2 medium red onions, sliced
olive oil to taste
1/2 teaspoon tarragon (optional)

DIRECTIONS

Cook beets in a pot of boiling water until done but still firm, about 30 minutes. Take skin off, and cut into crescent-shaped pieces.

Add onions to beets and mix with olive oil and tarragon.

STEAMED BROCCOLI WITH GARLIC, LEMON, AND OLIVE OIL

TIME: 30 MINUTES / SERVES: 6-8

A lovely vegetable, its taste and deep green color add a distinctive touch, especially when served with fish.

---

ingredients

3 bunches broccoli
3 garlic cloves
salt
juice of 3–4 lemons
3 tablespoons olive oil

DIRECTIONS

Steam broccoli, removing the hard part of the stalk and leaving good-sized florets intact.

Pound garlic cloves with several dashes of salt.

Add lemon juice and about 3 tablespoons of olive oil to the crushed garlic.

To serve, dip each floret in the garlic, lemon, and oil dressing and place on a platter. When finished, pour remaining dressing over the entire platter.

FOOLE
FAVA BEANS WITH OLIVE OIL

TIME: 1 HOUR+ / SERVES: 4-6

A filling side dish or even a basic lunch.

---

ingredients

1 pound dried fava beans
4–5 garlic cloves
juice of 2 lemons
1/2 cup olive oil
salt and pepper to taste

DIRECTIONS

Soak the fava beans in cold water overnight and one whole day. Rinse beans and put in a large pot of water. Bring to a boil and reduce heat. Cook until soft (45–60 minutes) and drain.

Pound 4–5 garlic cloves and add lemon juice.

Mix with fava beans, adding 1/2 cup olive oil.

Season with salt and pepper.

Optional: garnish with mint leaves and chopped red pepper.

TOFU AND KALE

TIME: 1 HOUR / SERVES: 4

---

ingredients

1 large bunch organic Tuscan kale
1 package plain organic tofu, firm or
    medium firm
3 medium to large yellow onions,
    sliced
1/4 to 1/2 cup olive oil
1/4 to 1/2 cup organic raw sunflower
    seeds
4 tablespoons organic tamari sauce, or
    to taste
3–4 carrots, chopped into large coins
    and steamed

DIRECTIONS

Wash kale well, remove ribs and stems (optional), and cut into small pieces.

Steam the kale until soft, about 30–40 minutes.

Sauté the onions over medium heat in olive oil until soft, about 5 minutes. Add the sunflower seeds and cook for 1 minute.

Add the steamed kale to onions and sunflower seeds and mix well.

Strain and cut the organic tofu into small pieces and add to the kale without mixing at first, letting the tofu heat up.

Add tamari sauce, mix all together, and cook for 5–10 minutes.

Serve on a platter with steamed carrots as a garnish for vivid color against the kale.

MEDITERRANEAN EGGPLANT

RECIPE BY
CHEF GEORGE NOUJAIM

TIME: 35 MINUTES / SERVES: 4-6

ingredients

1 large eggplant
1/2 cup olive oil
8 garlic cloves, chopped
1/2 cup cilantro, chopped
4 tomatoes, diced
1/4 cup Italian parsley, chopped
1 teaspoon pine nuts, toasted
salt and pepper to taste

DIRECTIONS
Preheat oven to 375°F.

Wash the eggplant and slice into rounds, leaving the skin on. Sprinkle with olive oil until the eggplant rounds are well coated. Roast in the oven on a sheet pan for 15 minutes.

Sauté the garlic in olive oil. Add the chopped cilantro and toss around for 30 seconds. Add the tomatoes, mix to combine. Allow to stew on low heat for 8 minutes.

Spread 2 tablespoons of the tomato stew over each of the eggplant rounds. Garnish with parsley and pine nuts.

Salt and pepper to taste.

BREADS & DESSERTS

"Mother had two categories of desserts. The regular ones she put on the table were really extensions of the main meal: fruits, rice pudding, a muffin with honey. Then there were the special, skillfully baked ones—ma'mool, macaroon kashab—reserved for birthdays and holidays. Were they ever worth waiting for! The mere aromas, followed by seeing dozens of them spread carefully on the kitchen table, turned us into Pavlovian specimens!"

MA'MOOL
PASTRY FILLED WITH CRUSHED PISTACHIO NUTS

TIME: 45 MINUTES, PLUS OVERNIGHT / MAKES 50-80 PASTRIES

Ma'mool is an exquisite light pastry filled with crushed pistachios. Not to be made when you are in a hurry. It uses an aromatic spice, mahlab, that is made from a small wild cherry pit.

---
ingredients for dough
---

2 cups baby farina or semolina
1 1/4 pound unsalted butter (clarified)
1 jigger (1–2 ounces) brandy (or whiskey)
1 1/4 teaspoon mahlab
1 yeast cube (2 tablespoons)
1 cup warm milk
4 cups unbleached white flour

---
ingredients for filling
---

1 pound unsalted pistachios or black walnuts or 1/2 pound of each (pistachios alone are preferred)
1 cup sugar, plus powdered sugar for topping
2 1/2 tablespoons orange blossom water (or rose water)

PREPARE DOUGH
Mix butter and farina or semolina the night before cooking.

To clarify butter, bring to a gentle boil and stir until there is no more foam on top. Salt will stick to the bottom of the pan. Strain the butter through a fine strainer over the farina. Stir and leave overnight. This dough does not rise.

When you're ready to make the ma'mool, beat farina/butter mixture for about 10 minutes until it turns creamy white. Add brandy and mahlab.

Dissolve yeast in warm milk, stirring. Add to farina mixture. Gradually add the flour to the mixture, mixing until the dough is smooth.

PREPARE THE FILLING
Coarsely grind the pistachios. Mix with sugar and orange blossom or rose water.

ASSEMBLING THE MA'MOOL
Preheat oven to 300°F.

Take a small amount of dough (approximately 1 tablespoon) and round it in the cradle of your hand; with a forefinger, core into the dough until it is in the shape of a small oval cup with thin sides. The ma'mool is more delicious if it has lots of filling. This is feasible if the cored hole is large and the sides of the cup are thin.

Put approximately a teaspoon of filling into the cup, and then gently seal the opening and face the closed opening into the palm of hand. Gently roll in hand until you have a rounded ball of dough. Repeat until all material is used.

Decorate top of ma'mool by pinching the soft dough with a pastry crisper or tweezers, again and again. A cookie mold designed to be gently pressed on the top can alternatively be used.

Bake for about 40 minutes, or until brown on the bottom and barely showing color on the top.

Sprinkle superfine powdered sugar on top of the hot ma'mool.

MACAROON KASHAB
GLAZED SESAME SEED MACAROONS

TIME: 4 HOURS / MAKES 90 MACAROONS

Although macaroons may be considered sweets, they serve as nourishment also. These macaroons themselves are not sweet, but the glaze balances the subtle tastes in the body of the macaroon.

ingredients for macaroons

1 or 2 .6-ounce cakes of yeast (2 for quicker results)
1 cup lukewarm milk
10 cups unbleached white flour
2 cups sesame seeds (optional: slightly toast in oven)
2 1/2 cups olive oil
5 eggs, whisked
4 tablespoons anise seed
1 tablespoon mahlab

ingredients for syrup

5 cups white sugar
1 1/2 cups cold water
juice of 2 lemons
1 1/2 tablespoons orange blossom water

PREPARE THE MACAROONS
Dissolve yeast cakes in milk.

In a large bowl, mix flour and sesame seeds. Thoroughly combine anise seed and mahlab in a blender together and add to the flour mixture.

Add olive oil and whisked eggs to flour mixture.

Knead all the ingredients well (but not hard) for about 15 minutes until the bowl is clean on the sides. The dough should be a little loose.

Cover and let the dough rise for 1 hour.

Preheat the oven to 400°F.

After the dough has risen, form 2 handfuls into a big, long, rounded shape on the worktable, about 2 feet long. Cut the dough into 1-inch pieces.

To form a macaroon, gently press each 1-inch piece against the grain on a flat cheese grater to create a pattern. Carefully roll the dough off the grater in one motion with the back of your fingers, forming a macaroon about the shape of a forefinger. Place onto a cookie sheet with the overlap facing down.

Bake for about 25 minutes. The macaroons are finished when slightly brown.

PREPARE SYRUP FOR GLAZE
While macaroons are baking, dissolve sugar and water. Add lemon juice. Bring to a boil, stirring constantly, and boil for 3–4 minutes. Add orange blossom water.

With a slotted spoon, dip cooked macaroons in hot syrup to glaze as soon as they are removed from the oven. Remove from glaze and place in a colander sitting in a larger bowl to permit the macaroons to drain slightly before being placed on a platter.

If macaroons are being stored for future eating, use wax paper between layers to prevent them from sticking to each other.

STUFFED HONEYDEW

TIME: 40 MINUTES / SERVES: 5-6

You can't lose with good ingredients.

---

ingredients

1 honeydew melon
1 1/2 cups cold water
2 one-ounce packages unflavored gelatin
3/4 cup brown sugar
juice of 2 grapefruits
juice of 2–3 lemons
juice of 4 oranges
1 eight-ounce package cream cheese

PREPARE MELON

Peel and core the honeydew, making a large enough hole in the top of the melon so you can scoop out the fruit in the form of melon balls, leaving enough fruit around the edges to form a melon shell. The shell will be used to hold the gelatin and fruit stuffing.

PREPARE GELATIN

Boil water, and pour over gelatin and brown sugar. Mix well and cool until the mixture begins to gel.

Juice lemons, grapefruits, and oranges and add to the gelatin, mixing well. You can also mix in the melon balls.

Put gelatin mixture in the shell of the honeydew and refrigerate.

PREPARE TOPPING

Blend the cream cheese until soft.

When the gelatin is firm, cover the outside of the honeydew shell with the cream cheese and slice for serving.

KA'AK
SWEET YEAST BREAD

TIME: 2 1/2 HOURS /
MAKES ABOUT 90 PIECES

Ka'ak are tasty and nutritious whether eaten with coffee or tea in the morning or as a snack with milk. My mother made them by the dozens, and they disappeared by the dozens!

---

ingredients for ka'ak

1 yeast cake (0.6 ounces)
1 quart milk
12 cups unbleached white flour
2 teaspoons mahlab
4 teaspoons anise seed
1 pound butter (clarified)
5 eggs

---

ingredients for glaze

2 cups of milk
3 tablespoons rose water
powdered sugar, for sprinkling

PREPARE THE KA'AK

Dissolve yeast in lukewarm milk. Blend flour, mahlab, and anise seed until powderlike. Add flour mixture to milk and yeast.

Clarify the butter by boiling it until there is no foam on the top and then strain the butter over the flour mixture. Add the unbeaten eggs. Mix all and knead well. Let rise about 45 minutes.

Once risen, take a handful of dough, and roll it out with your hands until dough is elongated and about 1 1/2 inches thick. Cut in pieces and form into doughnut shapes.

Bake at 400°F for 20 minutes, or until golden brown on bottom.

PREPARE THE GLAZE

Mix milk and rose water.

Glaze top of ka'ak with the milk/rose water mixture.

Then sprinkle powdered sugar over the top.

CREAM CHEESE GELATIN DELIGHT

TIME: 30 MINUTES (PLUS OVERNIGHT) / SERVES: 20

Everyone waited for this at Christmas once a year. Mother also served this on other special occasions and we continue the tradition. My niece Nadia Mille-ron prepared the gelatin pictured here.

---

ingredients

5 one-ounce packages unflavored gelatin
1 cup cold water
1 cup hot water
1 1/2 cups dark brown organic coconut sugar
juice of 4 lemons
juice of 6 oranges
juice of 3 grapefruits
2 twenty-ounce cans sliced pineapple
2 eight-ounce packages cream cheese
fresh strawberries, sliced

DIRECTIONS

Soak the gelatin in cold water, then add the hot water and dissolve well.

Add coconut sugar and stir well.

Mix citrus juices, unstrained, and add to gelatin mixture. Stir well.

Pour in a bowl and leave in the refrigerator overnight.

Mix gelatin, cream cheese, and pineapple in a blender (first set on chop and then on puree) in small amounts until all have been blended.

Fold into a cake pan (10 inches in diameter with a tube in the middle) and allow to sit for one day before serving.

Turn the dessert onto a platter. This takes quick but steady movements so the dessert slips onto the platter without breaking up.

Decorate with fresh strawberries in the opening at the center and over the top of the entire dessert.

Slice and serve as one would a cake.

APPLE CAKE

TIME: 1 HOUR 15 MINUTES / SERVES: 20

This apple cake recipe leaves a taste superior to apple pie because it is lighter.

---
ingredients for dough

1/4 cup butter
2 eggs
1 cup brown sugar
juice of 2 lemons
zest of 1 lemon
1 cup unbleached white flour
dash of salt

---
ingredients for filling
---

30 tart Granny Smith apples, peeled
  and thinly sliced
juice of 2 lemons
1 cup brown sugar
2 teaspoons cinnamon
1/4 teaspoon mace (or nutmeg)
1 tablespoon butter
1 egg

PREPARE THE DOUGH
Blend butter until creamy and then add eggs, brown sugar, lemon juice, lemon zest, flour, and a dash of salt.

Mix and knead well.

Divide the dough into two parts.

Sprinkle flour on worktable, and then roll out one part until very thin. Use a large 18" x 11" x 2" pan and cover with the thin layer of dough.

Bake this layer in a preheated 400°F oven for 7 minutes until it is lightly browned. Remove and reduce heat to 350°F.

PREPARE THE FILLING
Mix the apples with lemon juice, brown sugar, cinnamon, mace, and butter at room temperature.

Spread over the baked crust.

Roll out the second layer of dough and spread over the apples evenly until completely covered.

Beat egg and spread over the top crust.

Bake at 350°F until top is brown.

Serve plain, or with whipped cream or vanilla ice cream.

RICE PUDDING

TIME: 35 MINUTES / SERVES: 8

This is a simple, easy dessert that is particularly satisfying if one is under the weather.

---

ingredients

1 cup basmati rice, rinsed and drained
2 cups water
1 cup milk
2 tablespoons sugar
1 teaspoon rose water
1 teaspoon orange blossom water

DIRECTIONS

In a 3-quart pot, combine water and rice, bring to a boil uncovered, and reduce heat to simmer, cooking until rice is tender and water is absorbed (approximately 15–20 minutes).

Add milk, sugar, rose water, and orange blossom water. Cook until creamy, over low heat, stirring often.

Serve in individual glass bowls.

TWO-TWO-TWO COOKIES

TIME: 1 HOUR / MAKES ABOUT 30 LARGE COOKIES

My sister Claire baked the cookies pictured below.

ingredients

1/4 cup olive oil
4 eggs, beaten
1/3 cup maple syrup
1 teaspoon rose water
1 teaspoon orange blossom water
2 cups unbleached white flour
1 teaspoon baking powder
2 cups shredded coconut
2 cups raisins
1 teaspoon baking soda
2 cups wheat germ
2 cups walnuts, chopped

DIRECTIONS

Preheat oven to 350°F.

Mix olive oil, eggs, maple syrup, rose water, and orange blossom water.

Mix dry ingredients together, and then combine with the wet ones.

Take a teaspoon of cookie batter and form the cookies.

Place on a baking tray and bake for about 20 minutes, until golden brown.

CRUNCHY BRAN MUFFINS

TIME: 30 MINUTES / SERVES: 6-8

This recipe comes from the "lake country" in Ontario, Canada. We've greatly enjoyed this muffin over the years. My sister Claire baked the muffin pictured above.

ingredients

1 cup organic plain yogurt
1 teaspoon baking soda
1/4 cup butter, creamed
1/2 cup maple syrup
1 egg
1 tablespoon molasses
1 cup natural bran
1 cup unbleached flour
1/4 teaspoon salt
1/4 cup each raisins or currants, finely
  chopped nuts, and dates

DIRECTIONS
Preheat oven to 375°F.

Combine yogurt and baking soda and set aside.

Mix creamed butter and maple syrup thoroughly. Then add the egg and mix well.

Add the yogurt and baking soda mixture to the eggs and butter, then add in molasses and the bran and blend.

Stir in the flour and salt.

Fold in the fruits and nuts.

Spoon into well-greased muffin cups and bake until done, approximately 20 minutes, or until a toothpick inserted into the center of a muffin comes out clean. The muffins shrink while baking, making them easy to remove.

ZUCCHINI BREAD

RECIPE BY MY AUNT, ANGELE B. MOKHIBER

TIME: 30 MINUTES / SERVES: 16

Serve heated or at room temperature. May be refrigerated or frozen.

ingredients

3 cups unbleached white flour
1/2 cup wheat germ
1 cup organic brown coconut sugar
1/2 teaspoon baking soda
3/4 teaspoon baking powder
1 1/2 teaspoons cinnamon
1/2 teaspoon nutmeg
1 cup organic walnuts or pecans,
   chopped coarsely
1 cup raisins
4 eggs
1 cup olive oil
2 tablespoons orange blossom water
2 cups peeled and grated zucchini

DIRECTIONS

Preheat oven to 350°F.

Mix the dry ingredients.

Beat the eggs well and add the olive oil, orange blossom water, and the grated zucchini. Mix thoroughly.

Add the dry ingredients to the zucchini mixture and combine well.

Turn batter into 2 greased and floured loaf pans (ideally 9" x 5" x 2 3/4").

Bake 55–60 minutes, or until tester is inserted and comes out clean.

CONVERSIONS

1 teaspoon	5 ML	1 ounce	28 G
1 tablespoon or 1/2 fluid ounce	15 ML	4 ounces or 1/4 pound	113 G
1 fluid ounce or 1/8 cup	30 ML	1/3 pound	150 G
1/4 cup or 2 fluid ounces	60 ML	8 ounces or 1/2 pound	230 G
1/3 cup	80 ML	2/3 pound	300 G
1/2 cup or 4 fluid ounces	120 ML	12 ounces or 3/4 pound	340 G
2/3 cup	160 ML	1 pound or 16 ounces	450 G
3/4 cup or 6 fluid ounces	180 ML	2 pounds	900 G
1 cup or 8 fluid ounces or half a pint	240 ML		

1 1/2 cups or 12 fluid ounces	350 ML
2 cups or 1 pint or 16 fluid ounces	475 ML
3 cups or 1 1/2 pints	715 ML
4 cups or 2 pints or 1 quart	950 ML
4 quarts or 1 gallon	3.8 L

F Fahrenheit	C Celsius	F Fahrenheit	C Celsius
250	120	350	180
275	135	375	190
300	150	400	200
325	165	425	220

ACKNOWLEDGMENTS

I start with my parents, who provided the heritage of wonderful food, as well as my aunt, Angele B. Mokhiber, my mother's sister, who cooked wonderfully wholesome food for us whenever we visited and showered abundant hospitality on us in myriad ways (look for her zucchini bread recipe in this volume); my sisters, Claire and Laura, for continuing their food traditions, and Claire for her meticulous ways with this book; my nieces, Nadia and Rania Milleron, and my nephew, Tarek Milleron, who worked our venerable kitchen for our delights and memories; Chef George Noujaim, of Noujaim's Bistro, who prepared most of our recipes and added two favorites of his own; the recipe photographer, Wendy Pernerewski; and Jean Bauer for constant helpfulness in readying the manuscript for publication. Of course, credit is due to Johnny Temple, my publisher at Akashic Books, for his enthusiasm and advice, inspired by Greg Ruggiero and the early engagement of Joan Claybrook and John Richard.

INDEX

David Alfaya

102

RALPH NADER is one of America's most effective social critics. His analyses and advocacy have enhanced public awareness and increased government and corporate accountability. And his example has inspired a whole generation of consumer advocates, citizen activists, and public-interest lawyers. Nader first made headlines as a young lawyer in 1965 with his book *Unsafe at Any Speed,* a scathing indictment that lambasted the auto industry for producing unsafe vehicles. The book led to congressional hearings and the passage of a series of auto-safety laws in 1966. Nader also went on to found a wide variety of organizations, all aimed at advancing corporate and government accountability.

Groups founded or actively inspired by Nader include Public Citizen, the Center for Auto Safety, the Center for Science in the Public Interest, the Clean Water Action Project, the Pension Rights Center, Public Justice, Princeton Project 55, and the Appleseed Foundation—a nonprofit network of seventeen public interest justice centers. In addition, Nader conceived and enabled the creation of numerous public interest research groups (PIRGs), funded and directed by college students in over twenty states. He also played a pivotal role in advancing and improving several major federal consumer-protection laws, such as life-saving motor vehicle laws, the Safe Drinking Water Act, the Wholesome Meat and Wholesome Poultry inspection laws, the Clean Air and Clean Water Acts, the landmark Freedom of Information Act, historic whistleblower protections, disability rights legislation, and veterans' safeguards; and he worked tirelessly to launch federal regulatory agencies such as the National Highway Traffic Safety Administration (NHTSA), the Occupational Safety and Health Administration (OSHA), the Environmental Protection Agency (EPA), and the Consumer Product Safety Commission (CPSC).

An author, lecturer, attorney, and political activist, Nader was cited by the *Atlantic* in 2006 as one of the one hundred most influential figures in American history; *Time* magazine has called him the "US's toughest customer"; and in 1974, a survey conducted by *U.S. News & World Report* rated him as the fourth most influential person in the United States.

Nader is the author of many books, articles, and syndicated columns (see Nader. org), plus the podcast and radio broadcast, *The Ralph Nader Radio Hour.* He has shown time and again how one person can make a difference in America, and that achieving justice, with citizen determination, knowledge, and backing by public opinion, *is easier than we think!*

Rose B. Nader with her great-grandson Adnaan Stumo

"Rose Nader used family dinners as an opportunity to inform her children about culture, philosophy, as well as nutrition. Her tasty recipes came with a heaping helping of love and knowledge." —**Phil Donahue**

"Rose Nader not only prepared the cuisine of my family's homeland to perfection, she infused it with heritage. Whenever she brought me a magical plate of Lebanese goodies, she was sure to remind me, in Arabic, of that old motto of the Lebanese kitchen: An empty hand is a dirty hand."
—**Marlo Thomas,** actress, author of *Growing Up Laughing: My Story and the Story of Funny*